POET OF THE WORD
RE-READING SCRIPTURE
WITH
EPHRAEM THE SYRIAN

———◆———

ÆLRED PARTRIDGE OC

———◆———

SLG Press
Convent of the Incarnation
Fairacres, Parker Street
Oxford OX4 1TB
www.slgpress.co.uk

© 2020 SLG Press
First Edition 2020

Fairacres Publications No. 187

Print ISBN 978-0-7283-0303-4
ISSN 0307-1405

Edited and typeset in Palatino by Julia Craig-McFeely

SLG Press
Convent of the Incarnation
Fairacres Oxford
www.slgpress.co.uk

Printed by
Grosvenor Group Ltd, Loughton, Essex

ACKNOWLEDGEMENTS

My thanks are due to the many students of Saint Ephraem, especially Sebastian Brock, without whose painstaking scholarship this essay would have been impossible. Special thanks are also due to my editor, Dr Julia Craig-McFeely, whose editorial skills have transformed a difficult typewritten manuscript into a readable book. Any infelicities or errors that remain are solely the responsibility of the author.

CONTENTS

INTRODUCTION

THIS discussion of the biblical hermeneutics (the theory of inter-preting Scripture) of St Ephraem the Syrian began life as a brief essay written for the brothers of the Anglican Order of Cistercians. A central feature of our Cistercian charism is the traditional monastic manner of reading and meditating on the Bible known as *lectio divina* or Sacred Reading. It is a way of prayerfully reflecting on the texts of Scripture, whereby we lay aside our conventional manner of reading that tends to come to rest with the literal, surface references of the text, and permit our mind and imagination to enter into a deeper, richer, more imagistic or 'allegorical' engagement with its symbolic allusions and inter-textual references often called the *sensus plenior* (the Fuller Sense). *Lectio divina* is a more personal, contemplative way of reading, that leads us away from the mere search for religious knowledge and draws us ever deeper into the mystery of God.

This manner of reading the Scriptures was second nature to al-most all Patristic authors, and is particularly evident in the writings of the fourth-century Syriac Church Father, St Ephraem. As a theologian, Ephraem was dedicated to upholding the orthodox doctrines of the Church defined at the Council of Nicaea (AD 325); but Ephraem was also a poet keenly conscious of the beguiling and constraining effects of theological dogmas, and highly sensitive to the allusive mystery of God that lay embodied in the pages of Scripture beneath its literal references, that could only be gestured at in the paradoxical language of poetry. Hence, nearly all Ephraem's spiritual insights are presented as hymns, poetical homilies and commentaries. In his study of St Ephraem, *The Luminous Eye* (1992), Sebastian Brock, a con-temporary Syriac scholar and translator of Ephraem's writings, comments that Ephraem is 'continually urging the reader to move beyond the outer garment of words to the inner meaning and truth to which they point'. St Ephraem himself wrote, in a series of *Hymns on the Church*:

1

It is not at the clothing of words
that one should gaze,
but at the power hidden in words.[1]

Ephraem's writings remain an incomparable example of how to gaze at the 'power hidden' in the words of Scripture, and a sure guide to the Sacred reading of the Bible.

Feast of St Ephraem of Syria
June 9th 2020

---

[1] Quoted by Brock, *The Luminous Eye*, 161. He cites in his bibliography *Hymns of the Church* (fifty-two hymns): Corpus Scriptorum Christianorum Orientalium, 198–9/Scriptores Syri, 84–5 (German); English of no. 9 (by R. Murray) in *Sobornost incorporating Eastern Churches Review* 2 (1980), and of no. 36 (by Brock) in *Sobornost incorporating Eastern Churches Review* 7 (1976).

I

EPHRAEM THE SYRIAN

IN 1920 Pope Benedict XV declared the last theologian of the East to be honoured with the title 'Doctor of the Church'.[2] The theologian so honoured was St Ephraem the Syrian, who has been described as 'the most important representative of Syriac Christianity in its most semitic form' at a time when Greek philosophy and language were shaping Christian doctrine in other parts of the Church.[3] Yet, despite the differences of language and culture, Ephraem's thought is not so very far removed from his Cappadocian contemporaries, Basil the Great (*c.* 330–79), bishop of Caesarea in Cappadocia and organiser of monastic life in the East; his brother Gregory (*c.* 335–395), bishop of Nyssa and a theologian of great mystical depth; and Gregory of Nazianus (*c.* 329–390), bishop of Constantinople.[4]

Ephraem was born, as far as we can tell, in AD 306 in the Syrian city of Nisibis on the easternmost edge of the Roman Empire and lived here for more than fifty years. Situated some 130 miles to the east of the famed ancient city of Nineveh, Nisibis nestled among the foothills below the Masious Mountains and the nearby River Chaboras, a tributary feeding into the mighty Euphrates. Being a way station on the busy trade routes from the west of the Empire to Mesopotamia and beyond, Nisibis was an important commercial centre. Although the city seems to have been religiously and culturally diverse, it had a marked Jewish character that must have influenced the vibrant Syrian Christian intellectual and monastic presence that had developed by the fourth century.[5]

---

[2] Benedict XV proclaimed St Ephraem a Doctor of the Universal Church in an encyclical letter issued on 5 October 1920 ('Principi apostolorum Petro').

[3] 'Ephrem Syrus', in *A Dictionary of Christian Spirituality*.

[4] See 'Gregory of Nazianzus' in *A Dictionary of Christian Spirituality*.

[5] Hansbury, *Hymns of Saint Ephrem the Syrian*, 4.

Syrian monasticism at this time differed significantly in style from that which was becoming firmly established in the West, especially in the Egyptian Desert.[6] The distinctive Syrian manner of embracing an ascetic way of life seems to have been characterised by small groups of celibate men and women who had adopted some form of consecrated life-style, and were collectively known as 'virgins'. There was also another group of Christians referred to as 'holy' or 'sanctified': these were married couples who had renounced all conjugal relations. Together these two groups of dedicated men and women were given the title Children of the Covenant.

For most Christians at this time baptism was delayed to late adulthood, and it is probable that these Children of the Covenant took vows to live consecrated lives when they were baptised as adults. Sebastian Brock describes this style of asceticism as 'proto-monasticism'.[7] Unlike the predominantly eremitic ascetical culture that was a feature of Egyptian monasticism, by which men and women sought to isolate themselves in the wilderness in order to encounter God, these Syrian consecrated men and women immersed themselves in their local communities.[8]

David Bently Hart describes the impact of this style of Christian presence in Nisibis as a disciplined monastic community that fostered the study of philosophy and theology, as well as being renowned for the medical training of its clergy, who established schools and libraries, founded hospitals, and fostered healthcare.[9]

It was into this cultural milieu that Ephraem was born. Little is known of his life for certain. The legends woven into the accounts of

---

[6] See 'Desert Fathers', in *A Dictionary of Christian Spirituality*.

[7] Brock comments: 'Central to this ascetic tradition was the ideal lying behind the term *iḥidaya*, a word covering a whole variety of different meanings, 'single', 'celibate', 'single-minded', 'simple' (in the sense of straightforward), and most importantly 'a follower or imitator of Christ the *Iḥidaya*, or the "Only-Begotten"'. *Ephrem the Syrian: Hymns on Paradise*, 26.

[8] 'Syrian proto-monasticism was essentially an urban and village phenomenon.' Brock, *idem*, 25.

[9] Bently Hart, *The Story of Christianity*, 133.

4

his life by later biographers make it difficult to untangle authentic details from hearsay and fabrication. Many of these biographies have clearly been influenced by traditional hagiographical motifs. Common motifs, for example, are those that hint at a prenatal divine vocation, a holy childhood and revelatory dreams or visions. John Gwynn, in his assessment of Medieval biographies of Ephraem, cites an early tradition that despite his pagan environment, Ephraem was chosen 'like Jeremiah from his mother's womb' to spread the truth and to quench heresy. Ephraem was therefore preserved in his childhood 'from all taint of idolatrous worship and its attendant impurities'. The same biographer also recounts that as an infant Ephraem had a dream or vision of a vine emerging from his mouth that grew 'as to fill all that was under the heavens' and produced such an abundant harvest of grapes that the birds constantly fed on them and 'multiplied the more'. Ephraem himself, in a work known as his 'Testament', interprets the clusters of fruit as his Sermons and the leaves of the vine as his Hymns.[10]

A rare autobiographical allusion, however, in one of Ephraem's hymns seems to hint that both his parents were Christians.[11] Brock suggests some of Ephraem's hymn texts imply he was baptised at an early age. In Hymn 26 'Against Heresies' he states, 'I was born in the path of truth, even though my childhood was unaware'; in Hymn 37, 'On Virginity', Ephraem says: 'Your truth was with me in my youth.' Brock takes these verses as allusions to his baptism.[12] This interpretation has not convinced all scholars. Basing his evidence on early sources, John Gwynn states firmly that Ephraem's parents were non-Christian, and that his father was a priest of the pagan goddess Abinal or Abizal (presumably a Persian deity).

Our evidence suggests that Ephraem was only introduced to Christianity as a youth, and that he received his Christian education

---

[10] See Böer, *Hymns and Homilies of Ephraim the Syrian*, introduction by Gwynn, 13.

[11] See 'Ephraem (Ephrem, Ephraim), Saint' in *The Catholic Encyclopedia*, vol. 5; an idea contradicted by a later biography known as the *Syriac Life of Ephrem* (ed. Brockelmann), and that describes Ephraem's father as a pagan priest.

[12] Brock, *Ephrem the Syrian: Hymns on Paradise*, 9.

as one of the Catechumens under the care of James (or Jacob) the saintly Bishop of Nisibis, and was baptised at the age of eighteen (or twenty-eight, depending on his date of birth). At some point in his adult life Ephraem was ordained as a deacon and served as a catechetical teacher for a series of notable Syrian bishops until the last decade of his life.[13] He almost certainly acted as a choirmaster for one of the groups of female 'virgins', and wrote a number of hymn cycles while in Nisibis. Brock is clearly of the opinion that Ephraem spent much of his stay in Edessa by 'organising choirs of women to sing his specially-written hymns'.[14] Brock also comments that the largest proportion of his literary output dates from the last years of his life in Edessa.

Among his corpus of hymns are, for example: Hymns on Christ; Hymns on the Nativity; Hymns on Faith; Hymns on Paradise; Hymns on Virginity; Hymns on the Church; Hymns on the Unleavened Bread; Hymns for the Feast of the Epiphany; Funeral Hymns.[15]

Although there is no documented evidence that Ephraem was formally medically trained, Bently Hart describes the Catechetical School in Nisibis as 'one of the centres for medical training for which Nestorian Christian monks and missionaries were so justly renowned in subsequent centuries'.[16] In light of Ephraem's response to the healthcare crisis in Edessa, it is not unreasonable to speculate that he himself received or acquired some medical knowledge during his time in Nisibis.

During the years Ephraem resided in Nisibis the city was harassed by various Persian kings, who sought to annexe the city in order to expand their empire. There were a number of these sieges, but all were unsuccessful. One, though, deserves mention. In AD 350

---

[13] Brock lists these as: Jacob (Hames) *d.* 338; Babu *c.* 338–350; Vologeses *c.* 350–361; Abraham born *c.* 361.

[14] Brock, *Harp of the Spirit*, 9.

[15] For a bibliography of Ephraem's hymns available in English see Brock, *idem*, 159.

[16] Bently Hart, *The Story of Christianity*, 137.

the Persian ruler King Shapur II dammed the River Chaboras in order to flood the land surrounding the city. Although it failed to secure Nisibis, the event was dramatic enough for Ephraem to refer to it in one of the hymn collections he wrote at this time. He compares the city to Noah's Ark floating on the waters of the deluge. Nisibis personified declares:

> All kinds of storms trouble me
> and I count the Ark fortunate:
> only waves surround it,
> but ramps and arrows as well surround me ...
> O Helmsman of the Ark,
> be my pilot on dry land;
> You rested the Ark on the haven of a mountain,
> give rest to me too in the haven of my walls.[17]

Despite the failure of this tactic, thirteen years later the Persians finally achieved their goal. In AD 363, when Ephraem was fifty-seven years old, the Roman Emperor, Julian, was killed during a skirmish into Persian territory. As part of a negotiated peace treaty Nisibis was handed over to the Persians. Apparently, one of the conditions was that the Christian population should leave the city; Ephraem was among the numerous refugees who left Nisibis. Not long after, he settled in the city of Edessa, about 130 miles west of Nisibis, a city in which Christianity had long been established.

From the little we can garner from the time Ephraem spent living in Edessa, it is probable that he led a form of solitary ascetical life in one of the many caves that were to be found among the rocky outcrops in the hills close to the city, where both male and female anchorites sought retreat. Paul Böer describes this period in Ephraem's life as one in which he 'rose into repute as a teacher, and a champion against heresy; and no less as an ascetic and a saint'.[18]

---

[17] *Nisibene Hymns* 1:3. Translated in Brock, *The Luminous Eye*.
[18] See Böer, *Hymns and Homilies of St. Ephraim the Syrian*.

The last decade of Ephraem's life, spent in this semi-monastic way, was not without its practical challenges and social involvement.

Palladius, a fifth-century historian of early Christianity, recounts that in the summer of AD 372 the local wheat harvest that supplied the population of Edessa failed due to a year-long drought, resulting in a devastating famine. Because of his reputation as a holy man, the city fathers petitioned Ephraem to assist them in the crisis and help care for the starving and ailing residents. True to his vocation as a deacon, and with his medical training, Ephraem set about organising a sophisticated programme of healthcare. This included the provision of a 300-bed field hospital for those suffering from the effects of malnutrition, and dignified funerals for the dead. Palladius said of Ephraem's tireless efforts on behalf of the devastated city: 'he also had all those suffering from starvation in the villages brought in and given beds. He spent every day in constant attendance on them, seeing to their every need with great caring ... this he did joyfully'.[19]

The famine finally abated in the Spring of AD 373 when the barley crop was ready for harvesting in May. The next month, on June 9th, the Chronicle of Edessa announced Ephraem's death. He was 67 years old. The cause of his death is uncertain: he may have contracted an illness while caring for the sick of Edessa, or he may simply have been exhausted by the physical demands of caring for those he ministered to with such unstinting devotion. Clearly, Ephraem embraced selflessly the pastoral challenges of his ministry as a fundamental aspect of his Christian identity. What he has left us, however, as his abiding heritage, are his incomparable biblical commentaries written both in poetry and prose, and his poetic homilies and hymns. A significant number of these were written while Ephraem was resident in Edessa.

These poetic works, especially the hymns, echo the characteristically Semitic love of antithesis and parallelism so often found in the

---

[19] Brock, *Ephrem the Syrian: Hymns on Paradise*, 15. Brock comments that there is no reason to doubt the historical veracity of this narrative about Ephraem's involvement in the famine.

Psalms, and which in Ephraem's hands 'proves a tool admirably suited to the expression of the various paradoxes of the Christian mystery'.[20]

Brock speaks of Ephraem as a theologian-poet who combined a 'technical artistry with a richness of imagery that is at times breathtaking'.[21] Not all commentators have been as enthusiastic as Brock, however. The *Oxford Dictionary of the Christian Church* states rather disparagingly of Ephraem's hymns and sermons: 'Their inspiration is scriptural throughout, but their style, characterised by repetition and the accumulation of metaphors, is alien to most modern tastes'.[22] By contrast, Murray describes him as 'perhaps the greatest poet of the Patristic age and, perhaps, the only theologian-poet to rank beside Dante'.[23]

---

[20] Brock, *The Harp of the Spirit*, 7.

[21] *idem*, 7.

[22] 'Ephraem Syrus' in *The Oxford Dictionary of the Christian Church*.

[23] Murray, *Symbols of Church and Kingdom*, 31. Murray's book is a detailed study in some themes of early Syriac biblical exegesis.

II
EPHRAEM'S CONTEXT

IT appears that Ephraem's hymns and homilies had a liturgical setting; a good proportion of them being produced as choral
responses to the scripture lessons read in worship. Griffith states:
'The fact that so much of Ephraem's writing had a pastoral setting, a
good portion of it even being produced as choral response to the
scripture lessons in the liturgy, reminds one of the centrality of the
Bible in all of his work.'[24] In these hymns and homilies he was no less
an exegete than in the more traditional biblical commentaries associated with his name. Indeed, Jacob of Sarug, a fifth-century Syriac
writer, bears witness to Ephraem's reputation in his own verse
homily dedicated to him, in which he describes Ephraem as a skilled
composer of doctrinal hymns carefully crafted to commend right
teaching and refute error.[25] Ephraem's own theology was firmly
grounded in Nicaean orthodoxy and he wrote in particular with the
Arian heresy in mind.

Arianism was a Christological heresy condemned by the Council
of Nicaea (325), which derived from the teaching of an Alexandrian
priest, Arius (*c.* 250–*c.* 336). Although well-read theologically and
traditional in his thinking, he asserted that the person of the Son had
not always existed from eternity ('there was a time when he was
not') but had been created by God and consequently was not divine
by nature, although he was the first among creatures: his divinity
was only partial and derivative. It was a heresy that disturbed and
divided the early Church almost to the close of the fourth century.
The phrases in the Nicaean Creed 'begotten not made, and of one
substance [*homousios*] with the Father', were included to obviate his
trinitarian theology.

---

[24] Griffith, '*Faith Adoring the Mystery*', 13.

[25] *idem*, 6.

Perhaps the most significant theological ideas that impacted on Ephraem were those associated with Marcion, and his radical views about which scriptures were acceptable for Christians.

Marcion was a wealthy merchant who moved to Rome around AD 140. He was a prominent teacher in the local community and of such importance that almost every Christian writer in the second half of the second century wrote a book condemning his theology.[26] It would seem that Marcion had come under the influence of Gnosticism, a widespread Hellenistic form of mystical philosophy that was inherently dualistic.[27] It had emerged in the second century and drew on Jewish, Christian, and pagan sources, representing salvation as the freeing of spiritual elements from an evil material environment. Christian Gnostics denied the incarnation of Christ and rejected the tradition and scriptures of mainstream Christianity. In common with many established heresies, Gnostics claimed a privileged knowledge both of God and of human destiny arising from secret traditions and privileged revelations. Though Gnosticism was not a unified system of beliefs, its different expressions nevertheless had some common features. One of the focal beliefs was that the created world was fundamentally flawed and evil, and that salvation consisted in acquiring the mystical knowledge (*gnosis*) that had been revealed by a heavenly teacher and would provide those who acknowledge it a pathway back to their original divine origin and nature from which humankind had fallen into a disastrously defective cosmos.

Although Marcion was not a Gnostic in the full sense, these ideas clearly coloured his theology, and especially his evaluation of the Old Testament and the Jewish origins of Christian beliefs. He rejected the whole of the Old Testament as spiritually and theologically misleading and dangerous for Christians to use as a source of authentic revelation. In these Hebrew Scriptures Marcion found reflected an

---

[26] Unfortunately, none of these writings have survived except for an extended rebuttal by Tertullian (AD 159–225), in a book entitled *Against Marcion*.

[27] 'Gnosticism' in *A Concise Dictionary of Theology*. For a clear and accessible description of gnosticism see Tillich, *A History of Christian Thought*, 33ff.

image of a God who had created a World in which evil and corruption existed: a God who, in his relationship with mankind, often appeared to be wrathful and capricious. Marcion believed that a God of such character was wholly irreconcilable with the God of infinite love and mercy revealed in the life and teaching of Jesus. Marcion, therefore, drew a sharp distinction between what he perceived as two deities: the God of the Jews, whom he described as a lesser god, a demiurge, who was responsible for a flawed Creation, and the true God of Christian belief and devotion.[28]

Consequently, Marcion embarked on a programme of radical revision to remove any perceived Jewish influences in Christian writings in addition to his rejection of the Old Testament. His list of acceptable texts finally included an edited version of the Gospel of Luke (to remove certain sections that had a Jewish nuance) and a selection of the epistles of St Paul, also edited in places.

Marcion's anti-Jewish programme brought into sharp relief the pressing challenge for the early Church to define its relationship to its Jewish heritage, and how to embrace and interpret the Scriptures of the Old Testament that the majority of Christian theologians believed were a fundamental and integral part of their identity, and a profound deposit of doctrinal and spiritual illumination.

One Christian theologian who took up the challenge to refute Marcion was Origen, a youthful scholar and head of the catechetical school in Alexandria towards the end of the second century. In his Introduction to the classic study of Origen, Jean Daniélou explains that 'Origen's writings can be said to mark a decisive period in all fields of Christian thought. His researches into the history of the different versions of the Scriptures and his commentaries on the literal and the spiritual senses of the Old and New Testaments make him the founder of the scientific study of the Bible'.[29]

---

[28] Heine, *Reading the Old Testament with the Ancient Church*, 70–4 has an extended discussion of all aspects of Marcion's theology.

[29] Daniélou, *Origen*. Although now somewhat dated, Daniélou's book was

Origen was born about the year AD 185 into a Christian family living in the Egyptian city of Alexandria, a thriving metropolis that had become home to Hellenised Jews, Greek philosophers and scholars, and a variety of Christian teachers. Founded in the year 332 BC by Alexander the Great, by the end of the second century AD Alexandria had emerged as one of the leading cities of the ancient world. It had been perfectly sited to play a major role in the busy sea-going trade between the Mediterranean and the Orient. With two magnificent harbours abutting the Mediterranean Sea, and a third to the south on Lake Mereotis connected by canals to the River Nile and the Red Sea, all sea trade to the East passed through Alexandria, hugely prospering the local economy.

The city also boasted a library of over 700,000 books, making it probably the most important resource for knowledge and learning in the known world. By the time of Origen Alexandria was the foremost centre for the study of philosophy and science. It was a hub for various schools of religious thought and speculation and home to a large Jewish population. One member of this community who was particularly influential was Philo (c. 20 BC–AD 50), a distinguished Jewish writer. Philo was intent on presenting Jewish Scriptures to a sophisticated Hellenised audience in a way that rendered them intellectually respectable and consistent with the prevailing philosophical ideas, especially those deriving from Plato. Philo applied to the interpretation of the Jewish Scriptures the allegorizing method used by Greek grammarians when seeking to make morally-unacceptable behaviour or gross nonsense in the texts of Homer intellectually respectable. The allegorical mode took the route of pointing beyond the surface meaning of a text by recognising a more profound, mystical or morally-edifying lesson hidden within it. Philo's hermeneutics of the the Jewish Scriptures were highly influential and made a lasting impact on the way subsequent Christian teachers interpreted the Old Testament.

---

the first major contemporary study of Origen's life and theology. The standard work is now that by Crouzel.

We know that Origen spent a significant period of his life in Antioch, where he wrote many of his biblical commentaries under the patronage of the empress Julia Mammaea. His distinctive style of exegesis quickly became influential. John McGuckin has commented:

> His influence was as great as that of Augustine in the West although in the Greek-speaking world the variety of other major thinkers moderating and redirecting the channels of his thought (such as Gregory of Nazianzus or Maximus the Confessor) ensured that his intellectual legacy would be more creatively received and developed.[30]

It is interesting that Gregory Nazianzus was closely associated with Gregory of Nyssa, who produced the encomium on Ephraem.[31] Ephraem's poetic corpus might be seen as an example of the way Origen's legacy was 'creatively received and developed' within a Syrian context.

Origen was clearly one of those theologians who benefitted from the hermeneutical ideas that filtered down from Philo's seminal writings. His father, Leonides, was himself a teacher of rhetoric and grammar (literary theory and criticism).[32] Leonides, we are told, recognised his son's academic and spiritual potential at an early age, immersing him in a daily study of the Scriptures and providing him with the best classical education available, at which Origen excelled.

Origen's youthful idyll was blighted, however, when in AD 202, when he was only seventeen, his father was arrested during an anti-Christian persecution and sentenced to death. Origen suddenly found

---

[30] McGuckin, 'Origen of Alexandria'.

[31] Gwynn, *Hymns and Homilies of St. Ephraim the Syrian*, 17.

[32] My use of the term 'literary theory' might be pushing an analogy too far, but in describing Origen's approach to biblical interpretation, Brian Daley SJ comments: 'Origen's peculiar genius, as the first professional Christian Scripture scholar we know of, was to do this mainly through direct biblical interpretation, in a way carefully anchored in the text, but also making use of the philosophical suppositions, the techniques of literary criticism … that so engaged Alexandrian intellectuals.' Daley, *God Visible: Patristic Christology Reconsidered*, 83.

himself responsible for supporting his mother and siblings as all Leonides's property had been confiscated by the state.[33] In order to provide for his family, Origen set himself up as a private tutor teaching Greek classics and literary criticism. He soon developed a reputation for his teaching of Christian beliefs. During this time he pursued his own studies in Greek philosophy—especially those ideas associated with the writings of Plato, which were becoming intellectually fashionable through the writings of the contemporary re-interpreters of Plato's ideas known as Neoplatonists.

Origen also came under the influence of prominent Christian teachers in Alexandria, in particular Clement, the head of the local Christian catechetical school. Clement (c. AD 150–215) was a Christian philosopher born in Athens, who became head of the Christian catechetical school in Alexandria some time around the year AD 180. Although only fragments of his writings survive, it is clear that he sought to present Christian theology as intellectually respectable in the wake of both Jewish and pagan critics, by demonstrating that Christian beliefs were consistent with the highest philosophical ideals of the time. Although Clement was above all a man of Scripture and the Apostolic Tradition, he was also firmly convinced that pagan philosophy was of divine origin. Like the earlier Christian writer, Justin, who had engaged both Jewish and pagan critics, Clement taught that all rational thought, wherever it was found, was a reflection of the divine Reason (or *Logos*). Though not of equal status as the Old Testament, God in his Providence had inspired Greek philosophers as a preparation for receiving the Gospel in a similar way to that by which the Torah and the Prophets prepared the Jews for the Incarnation of his Son—the *Logos* made flesh.[34]

---

[33] There is a charming anecdote, that when Origen's father had been arrested, in a youthful expression of filial devotion, Origen was keen to follow his father and undergo a martyrs' death beside him. Fortunately, his mother being more practical and deciding that losing her husband was quite enough, hid all Origen's clothes. Teenage modesty it seemed prevailed over religious zeal, and Origen remained safely at home.

[34] See Campenhausen, *The Fathers of the Greek Church*, 25–37, for a fuller description of Clement's teachings.

Clement was a major player in the sharp dialogues between Jewish and pagan opponents of Christianity. In his theological rebuttals of Christian critics, Clement was eager to defend Christian beliefs as neither irrational nor intellectually unsophisticated.

When Clement himself became a victim of another round of persecutions and was forced to flee from Alexandria, the local bishop, Demetrius, aware of Origen's reputation, asked him to take over the role of the head of the catechetical school. Although not yet eighteen years old, Origen took up the role with enthusiasm and put all his rigorous academic learning into defending the orthodox teachings of the Church.[35]

Origen was without doubt the most prolific early Christian writer. No one knows for certain the number of books, etc. that he wrote. St Jerome, writing two hundred years later, recorded that he had seen a list of Origen's works in the library at Caesarea numbering over two thousand. This may be an exaggeration, and the list of over eight hundred he mentions in one of his letters more realistic.[36]

Such writings were honed in rigorous debates with Jewish scholars, pagan philosophers, and Christian doctrinal minorities in a similar manner to that in which earlier Christian apologists had engaged with secular critics and theological opponents. What distinguished Origen, however, was his ability to bring together many of these theological arguments and reflections into an integrated and philosophically sophisticated description of Christian beliefs. His book *De Principiis* ('On First Principles') is the first serious attempt to write a work of systematic theology that covered all aspects of Christian thought. It covered the entire range of Origen's Christian vision and treated of God and heavenly beings (angels); the origin of the material world and the true nature of human beings; free will and its consequences (the Fall); Redemption by Christ and the interpretation of Scripture.

---

[35] D'Ambrosio, *Who Were the Church Fathers?*, 88–90. For a detailed study of Origen's desire to provide a solid intellectual foundation for Christian theological refection see Heine. *Origen: Scholarship in the Service of the Church.*

[36] Saint Jerome, Letter 30 to Paula, cited in D'Ambrosio, *Who Were the Church Fathers?*, 92.

Von Campenhausen observes: 'The new element which Origen gave to the Church was primarily the great systematic summary. He was responsible for the change from an occasional and superficial interest in philosophy to a methodological study of intellectual problems, from the aphorism of educated discussion to the responsible construction of a well-established theological system.'[37] Although Origen drew on the tradition of the Church and the reflections of previous early Church thinkers, some of his theological speculations were seen as too radical and led ultimately to the wholesale destruction of his writings in later decades, an incomparable loss to Christian scholarship.

For our purposes, however, it is Origen's biblical hermeneutics, especially of the Old Testament, that are of most relevance to an appreciation and understanding of the work of St Ephraem.

The most important fact about Origen was that he was, first and foremost, a pioneer in every aspect of biblical scholarship. He wrote commentaries and homilies on almost all of the books of the Bible, and among those that have survived on the Old Testament are homilies on Genesis, Exodus, Leviticus and Numbers.

As a scholar trained in the classical discipline of literary criticism and textual analysis, Origen was keenly aware of the importance of establishing as far as possible the original wording of an historical, especially sacred, text before entering into any interpretative dialogue with it. Origen therefore undertook the major project of producing the first parallel text of the Old Testament. Called the *Hexapla*, it consisted of the Greek translation of the Old Testament current in Alexandria and known as the Septuagint, alongside the Hebrew text and four additional Greek versions. 'In the matter of sheer detail they are not inferior to any modern commentary. The interpretation of the Gospel according to St John (as far as Chapter xiii, verse 33) covers no less than thirty-two 'volumes'. The explanation of the first six words, "In the beginning was the Word", required a whole volume.'[38]

---

[37] Von Campenhausen, *The Fathers of the Greek Church*, 42.
[38] *idem*, 47.

In the first instance, Origen was always concerned to understand the literal, surface meaning of biblical texts, and frequently referred to the unique exegetical resource of the *Hexapla*.

Yet, however important the grammatical integrity of the biblical text and its literal meaning remained for Origen, the ultimate issue for him was how to interpret and articulate the Jewish Scriptures to sophisticated Gentile converts that rendered them as both intellectually respectable and morally palatable. Many of the passages in the Old Testament, when read literall,y appeared to be naive, irrational, ethically repulsive, or sheer nonsense given the scientific outlook at the time.

For example, when commenting on the Creation and Paradise stories in the Book of Genesis, Origen wrote:

> Who that has understanding will suppose that the first, and second, and third day, and the evening and the morning, existed without a sun, and moon and stars? ... And who is so foolish as to suppose that God, after the manner of a husbandman, planted a paradise in Eden towards the east and placed in it a Tree of Life, visible and palpable, so that one tasting the fruit with the bodily teeth obtained life? And again, that one was a partaker of good and evil by masticating what was on a Tree? And if God is said to walk in the paradise in the evening, and Adam to hide himself under a tree, I do not suppose that anyone doubts that these things figuratively indicate certain mysteries, the history having taken place in appearance, and not actually ...[39]

The significant comment here is clearly: 'I do not suppose that anyone doubts that these things figuratively indicate certain mysteries, the history having taken place in appearance, and not in actuality ...' This observation defines Origen's hermeneutical programme. Although Origen took great pains to establish the literal, historical, superficial meaning of the biblical texts—even going so far as to learn Hebrew— his more pressing intention was to enable educated Christians to be able to read the Bible, especially the Old Testament, in such a way that

---

[39] Butterworth, *Origen, De Principiis* [On First Principles], Book IV, i:17.

they could learn to discern the 'certain mysteries' that lay hidden beneath its surface obscurities. In fact, Origen was convinced that morally-uncomfortable or philosophically-awkward passages in the Scriptures had been deliberately introduced by God to alert the mature Christian reader to the rich seams of spiritual insights waiting to be mined beneath the literal surface. It is by meditating upon these 'certain mysteries' hidden within the Word of God that the prayerful and spiritually-aware Christian begins to contemplate and comprehend the eternal mysteries that illuminate the entire shape and goal of their life. Origen, therefore, set about the task of formulating a manner of interpreting the Scriptures that would provide Christian readers with a trustworthy guide; building on the insights of earlier Church Fathers, Origen developed his unique approach.

Manlio Simonetti, analysing Origen's approach to scriptural exegesis in relation to earlier forms of Patristic biblical interpretation, states:

> If they are taken together one by one, almost all the characteristics of Origen's exegesis, from the distinction of several messages in Scripture to the allegorical evaluation of Hebrew names and the symbolism of numbers, can be found in exegetes who preceded him (especially Clement). But compared to his predecessors, Origen organised and systematised these more-or-less traditional features, using an incomparably superior knowledge of the actual biblical text ... In short, Origen made biblical hermeneutics into a real science, and, in that sense, he conditioned decisively all subsequent patristic exegesis.[40]

Origen began by establishing three pillars upon which his hermeneutics were erected. The first pillar was the fundamental conviction that *all* Scripture was inspired. Origen believed that the Word of God, the *Logos,* who had become incarnate in the human person of Christ, was the same Word that dwelt in the human words of the Bible and shines through them. Therefore, all of Scripture leads us into an encounter with Christ. Marcellino D'Ambrosio comments:

---

[40] Simonetti, *Biblical Interpretation in the Early Church,* 39.

Following the tradition that had been handed down to him, Origen believed that Scripture is God-breathed, or inspired by the Holy Spirit. For him, Biblical inspiration did not mean only that the human authors were inspired, but rather that the text is inspired. The Bible is full of the Spirit; the Spirit continues to dwell in the texts as in a temple. Origen was well aware that there were many human authors of the books and that they wrote in many different styles. But since they were all inspired by the same Spirit, all the books are held together and made alive just as the soul holds the body together and animates it.[41]

Origen's second pillar in the architecture of his hermeneutics was his unshakeable belief in the face of both Jewish and pagan critics, that the the Old Testament and the writings of the Evangelists and Apostles formed together a coherent and unified picture of God's revelation of himself in Creation, in the history of Israel and proclamation of the Prophets. Although the various books that make up the Bible when read individually often appear like discordant musical phrases out of tune with one another, Origen sought to attune readers to the harmonious whole and to recognise the leitmotif of the Person of Christ present on every page of the score. Origen's classical education provided the final pillar. Like almost all early Patristic writers, Origen accepted without question the validity of philosophical reasoning in the pursuit of truth.

In his endeavour to highlight the spiritual dimension behind the apparent outward meaning of the biblical text, Origen often used a biological metaphor, describing the literal meaning of the text as the 'body', and the inner meaning as the 'soul and spirit': the 'soul' corresponded to the moral lesson in Scripture, and the 'spirit' to the meaning for the Church and the understanding of Christian doctrine and the mystery of God.[42]

Origen's biblical hermeneutics have often been referred to as allegorical and censured for being overly subjective. In reality, however,

---

[41] D'Ambrosio, *Who Were the Church Fathers?*, 96.

[42] For a very detailed study of Origen's hermeneutical language of body, soul and spirit, see Lauro, *The Soul and Spirit of Scripture within Origen's Exegesis.*

his biblical interpretations were firmly based in the tradition of typological exegesis, where a figure or event in the Old Testament is read as a redactive lens over the New Testament mystery to which it is related.[43] Origen sought always to be an exegete of the Scriptures within the boundaries of 'the Rule of Faith' and orthodox theology as it was at this time defined. Unfortunately, many less insightful exponents of his approach to the Bible took the allegorical method to extremes and eventually brought Origen into disrepute.

However, Origen's nuanced and profound guide to reading the Sacred Scriptures became the standard approach for all Christian exposition of the Bible during the Patristic era, and influenced theologians both in the West and in the East.

Ephraem and Origen shared the same flexible and non-dogmatic approach to interpreting the mysteries contained within the Sacred Texts. But whereas Origen presented them in the measured and restrained prose of a philosopher, Ephraem wrote as a poet using scriptural symbols in a cascade of allusions, rather than following the linear schematic sequence of Greek thought. In *Hymns on Paradise II* for example, Ephraem takes some of the images that he often employs—the Ark, Moses and Paradise—and weaves them into a complex tapestry of allusions:

> Noah made the animals live
>   in the lowest part of the Ark;
> in the middle part
>   he lodged the birds,
> while Noah himself, like the Deity,
>   resided on the upper deck.
> On Mount Sinai it was the people
>   who dwelt below,

---

[43] See further the following well-known examples of biblical types and typological exegesis: 1 Pet. 3:20–21 (the Ark as a type of Baptism); John 3:14 (the Serpent as a type of Christ's Crucifixion); Matt. 12:38–41 (Jonah as a type of Christ's Death and Resurrection). See also Paul's use of typological exegesis in Gal. 4:21–31.

the priests round about it,
    and Aaron halfway up,
while Moses was on its heights,
    and the Glorious One on the summit.

A symbol of the divisions
    in that Garden of Life
did Moses trace out in the Ark
    and on Mount Sinai too;
he depicted for us the types of Paradise
    with all its arrangements:
harmonious, fair and desirable
    in all things—
in its height, in its beauty,
    its fragrance, and its different species.
Here is the harbour of all riches,
    whereby the Church is depicted.[44]

---

[44] Trans. Brock, *Hymns on Paradise*, 89.

III
EPHRAEM'S SCHOLARSHIP

ALTHOUGH there are scholarly debates surrounding the authenticity of a number of biblical commentaries that have been traditionally ascribed to Ephraem, most modern scholars accept as genuine his commentaries on Genesis and Exodus and a number of New Testament books which survive only in Armenian translations. His oft-quoted commentary on Tatian's *Diatessaron*[45] is, however, no longer regarded as directly from Ephraem's pen, but to have originated from within the catechetical school in Nisibis of which he was probably a choirmaster.

Nonetheless, there is a passage in the commentary on the *Diatessaron* which aptly sums up Ephraem's own approach to the scriptures and their interpretation. It reads:

Many are the perspectives of his word, just as many are the perspectives of those who study it. [God] has fashioned his world with many beautiful forms, so that each one who studies it may consider what he likes. He has hidden in his word all kinds of treasures so that each one of us, wherever we meditate, may be enriched by it. His utterance is a tree of life, which offers you blessed fruit from every side. It is like that rock which burst forth in the desert, becoming spiritual drink to everyone from all places. 'They ate spiritual food and drank spiritual drink'. (1 Corinthians 10:3–4)

---

[45] The *Diatessaron* was a collated version of the four Gospels to create a continuous narrative, compiled by Tatian *c.* AD 150–160. It circulated widely in Syriac-speaking countries, where it became the standard text until it gave way to the four separate Gospels in the fifth century. Its original language was probably Syriac or Greek. Tatian himself was a native of Syria who became a Christian in Rome in the mid-second century.

Therefore, whoever encounters one of its riches must not think that that alone which he has found is all that is in it, but rather that it is this alone that he is capable of finding from the many things in it. Enriched by it, let him not think that he has impoverished it. but rather let him give thanks for its greatness, he that is unequal to it. Rejoice that you have been satiated, and do not be upset that it is richer than you ... Give thanks for what you have taken away, and do not murmur over what remains and is in excess. That which you have taken and gone away with is your portion and that which is left over is also your heritage.[46]

In common with early Greek Fathers like Origen (and Gregory of Nyssa),[47] Ephraem's biblical exegesis is essentially creative. For Ephraem, inspiration was not a presence of the Spirit that enlightened only the original authors of the sacred texts, but is, rather, a continuing process, and one that affects every reader who is attentive to the hidden presence behind the words as he reads them. Ephraem writes:

> The Scriptures are laid out like a mirror,
> And the person whose inner eye is pure
> Sees therein the image of Divine Reality.[48]

Ephraem also warned against a purely literalist interpretation of biblical texts, which he sees as spiritually deadening.

Ephraem's approach has been characterised as a 'much needed antidote' to the theological tradition that is primarily concerned with providing precise theological definitions and firm boundaries to the use of theological language. Indeed, Ephraem considered

---

[46] McCarthy, 'Saint Ephrem's Commentary on Tatian's Diatessaron', 49–50.

[47] Gregory of Nyssa (c. 330–95), one of the Cappadocian Fathers, and influenced by Origen's approach to the task of biblical exegesis, is remembered especially for his *Life of Moses*, through which he presents a vision of the Christian's spiritual journey in the imagery of the Exodus, the wilderness wanderings and final inheritance of the Promised Land. It is a wonderfully nuanced and profound 'spiritual' reading of an Old Testament narrative.

[48] *Hymns on Faith* 67:8 trans. Brock, *The Luminous Eye*, 47.

such limited literal or dogmatic readings as potentially blasphemous since they tend to diminish or erode our experience of the utter mystery of God, who transcends all our attempts to describe him in literal language. Boundaries limiting our individual insights in our reception of the message of Scripture have a 'deadening and fossilizing' effect that obscures and distorts our immediate personal experience of God, who is encountered in the sacred texts as a mystery beyond all limits and definitions.[49]

Ephraem writes:

> He clothed Himself in our language, so that He might clothe us
> in his mode of life. He asked for our form and put this on,
> and then, as a father with His children, He spoke with our
> childish state.
>
> It is our metaphors that He puts on—though He did not
> literally do so;
> He took them off—without actually doing so: when
> wearing them,
> He was at the same time stripped of them.
> He puts on what is beneficial, then strips it off in exchange
> for another;
> the fact that He strips off and puts on all sorts of metaphors
> tells us that the metaphor does not belong to His true Being:
> because that Being is hidden, He has depicted it by means of
> what is visible.[50]

As a poet, Ephraem is keenly aware of the limitations of our human language when speaking of divine mysteries. If we are to speak of God at all, we have, as it were, to empty our familiar language of its limited human content and associations and allow it to take on a new and unfamiliar role in referring to the unfathomable mystery

---

[49] See Brock, *idem*, 23f.
[50] *Hymns on Paradise II* 31:1–2, trans. Brock, *idem*, 60–1.

of God. Ephraem sees in our human language, and especially in the language of Scripture, a kind of *kenosis*, a self-emptying by which God allows himself to be described in the limits of human language and rhetoric.

If we are to read the Scriptures with understanding, we must recognize that they are a wholly inadequate vehicle to express the depths of the divine mystery in their literal form, and the reader who would understand their spiritual treasures must learn how to dig beneath the surface:

> If someone concentrates his attention solely
> on the metaphors used of God's majesty,
> he abuses and misrepresents that majesty
> by means of those metaphors with which God has clothed
>   himself for man's own benefit,
> and he is ungrateful to that Grace
> which bent down its stature to the level of man's childishness:
> although God had nothing in common with it
> He clothed himself in the likeness of man
> in order to bring man to the likeness of himself.
> Do not let your intellect be disturbed by mere names,
> for Paradise has simply clothed itself in terms that are familiar
>   to you:
> it is not because it is poor that it has put on your imagery,
> rather, your nature is far too weak to be able
> to attain to its greatness, and its beauties are much diminished
> by being depicted in the pale colours that you are familiar with.[51]

Ephraem guards against a literalist interpretation of the sacred texts: these are clothed in metaphors and 'pale colours'. They are constrained by the limitations of human language and rhetoric, and only reveal their riches as we recognise and respond to a more imagistic and poetic reading of them.

---

[51] *Hymns on Paradise II* 6–7, trans. Brock, *Harp of the Spirit*, 13.

In particular, Ephraem relies on a typological reading of the Bible. The terms 'symbol' (the Syriac word he uses literally means 'mystery') and 'type' recur throughout his exegetical poetry. Sebastian Brock goes as far as to state:

> Perhaps no other writer has ever put typological exegesis to such creative use, employing it to provide an intricate network of links between the two Testaments, between this world and the heavenly world.[52]

Ephraem's reading of Scripture creates a rich tapestry of interrelated themes and symbolic associations that work on two separate planes: horizontally between the Old Testament and the New; and vertically between this world and heaven. In both cases, they serve to 'uncover' something of the 'hiddenness' of a mystery not yet fully revealed;[53] as St Paul termed it, 'seeing through a glass darkly' (1 Cor. 13:12). In a striking image, Ephraem depicts Christ mixing the symbols from Scripture and nature like coloured pigments to paint his own portrait.

> Scattered symbols you have gathered up
>   from the Torah for your comeliness.
> You have published the models ...
>   which are in your Gospel,
>   along with the prodigies and signs of nature.
> You have mixed them together as the paints for
> your portrait; you have looked at yourself,
> and painted your own portait.[54]

Echoing the exegetical tradition of the early Fathers, Ephraem locates the key to uncovering the hidden meanings in a Christological reading of the Old Testament embedded in its figurative language: especially in the names and titles ascribed to God, through which he

---

[52] Brock, *idem*, 13.

[53] Brock, *The Luminous Eye*, 23–9.

[54] *Hymns on Virginity* 28:2, trans. by Griffith, *'Faith Adoring the Mystery'*, 31

makes himself known. Ephraem cautions his readers to be particularly alert to their associations and resonances in what he calls 'the crucible' of the scriptures:

> Contemplate in his crucibles,
>   his names and his distinctions.
> For he has names,
>   perfect and exact;
> he also has names
>   metaphorical and transient ...
> Have a care for his names,
>   perfect and holy,
> for if you deny one
>   they will all fly away.
> They are tied to one another
>   and they carry all,
> like the pillars
>   of the world.[55]

These symbols, types, names and titles are the alchemical elements in the crucible of the text that enables spiritual gold to come into being. Or, to use Ephraem's metaphor, they are 'a bridge and a gate' that lead us into the 'luminous heights' of Paradise.[56] These verses from Hymn 5, in which Ephraem describes his response to reading the book of Genesis, encapsulate the spirit of his hermeneutical strategy:

> I read the opening of this book
>   and was filled with joy,
> for its verses and lines
>   spread out their arms to welcome me;
>
>   ...

---

[55] *Hymns on Faith* 44:1–3, trans. Wickes, *St. Ephrem the Syrian: The Hymns on Faith,* 240.

[56] *Hymns on Paradise* 9:20, trans. Brock, *St. Ephrem the Syrian; Hymns on Paradise,* 104.

and when I reached that verse
   wherein is written
the story of Paradise,
   it lifted me up and transported me
from the bosom of the book
   the very bosom of Paradise.
The eye of the mind
   travelled over the lines
as over a bridge, and entered together
   the story of Paradise

...

Both the bridge and the gate
   of Paradise
did I find in this book.
   I crossed over and entered;
my eye remained outside
   but my mind entered within.[57]

For Ephraem the figurative language of the Old Testament (in its broadest sense) is to be read, as are the narratives of the patriarchs and prophets, through the lens of the incarnate Word, and thus it comes to shape the Christian experience. Ephraem frequently refers to the 'mystic symbols' (*raze*, in Syriac), a term that includes both the senses of the Greek terms 'type' and 'mystery', but which are given a more extended meaning in Syriac. A 'symbol' for Ephraem was not merely a conventional linguistic sign; rather a *raza* is a pointer to a spiritual reality to which it not only gestures, but in which it 'actually participates in some sense'. In this way a symbol both enhances and validates the reality to which it points.[58] One is reminded of Paul Tillich's assertion that symbols participate in the reality to which they point. Commenting on this observation, David Soper writes: 'Protestantism has often reduced essential symbols, with their inherent numinous power, to accidental signs;

---

[57] Brock, *idem*, 102–4.

[58] Cf. Brock, *Treasure-house of Mysteries*, 18.

it has therefore tended to replace them with rationalism, moralism and emotionalism.'[59]

Ephraem's approach has therefore sometimes been referred to as 'symbolic theology' and contrasted with more discursive and philosophical modes of reflection. It is, therefore, important to have a clear idea of Ephraem's understanding of typological exegesis if we are to be able fully to appreciate his reading of the Bible and its poetic expression.

Although 'typological' readings of the scriptures were familiar to the Antiochene school of biblical interpretation, as a contemplative exercise the role of symbols, types names and titles had a far greater significance and application for Ephraem. For him they provide the very idiom of our theological grammar. The figurative language of the scriptures is the way in which God manifests his hidden reality in a manner that can be grasped by the human intellect. Theology consists in the contemplation of these mystic symbols through which God allows himself to be known. As Ephraem frequently wrote, God's revelation of himself is through a rhetoric of *kenosis*, foreshadowed in the Old Testament but embodied in Christ, who is God's rhetoric made flesh.

Ephraem's typological exegesis is richly-textured and imaginative and admits of multiple readings of every scriptural passage:

> If there were [only] one meaning for the words [of Scripture] the first interpreter would find it, and all other listeners would have neither the toil of seeking nor the pleasure of finding. But every word of our Lord has its own image, and each image has many members, and each member possesses its own species and form. Each person hears in accordance with his capacity, and it is interpreted in accordance with what has been given to him.[60]

Although Ephraem nowhere discusses the principles of his hermeneutics, his approach is everywhere evident: he begins with the

---

[59] Soper, *Major Voices in American Theology*.

[60] McCarthy, 'Saint Ephrem's Commentary on Tatian's Diatessaron', 139.

literal meaning of the text and then searches for the spiritual sense encoded in the symbols, types, names and figurative language which have Christ as their point of reference.

Ephraem, in company with the majority of church Fathers, perceived the presence of Christ, albeit incognito, lying behind the events and symbols of the Jewish scriptures that they had inherited. Brock comments, 'Not surprisingly the vast majority of types and symbols Ephrem discovers latent in the Old Testament point forward to the advent of Christ: what was hidden in the symbol is revealed in Christ.'[61] Griffith comments that for Ephraem there is an integral unity between the Old and New Testaments (the Christian Bible) which 'has Christ as its focal point'.[62] In *Hymns on Faith*, for example, Ephraem sees in the story of Noah a symbol (or 'mystery') not only of baptism, but also a pointer to Christ's Crucifixion:

> Noah's Ark marked out by its course the sign of its Preserver,
> the Cross of its Steersman and the Wood of its Sailor
> who has come to fashion for us a Church in the waters of baptism:
> with the three-fold name He rescues those who reside in her,
> and in place of the dove, the Spirit administers her anointing
> and the mystery of her salvation. Praise to her Saviour.
> His symbols are in the Law, His types are in the ark,
> each bears testimony to the other: just as the ark's recesses
> were emptied out, so too the types in Scripture
> were emptied out; for by His coming he embraced
> the symbol of the Law, and in His churches He brought to completion
> the types of the ark.[63]

This does not, however, lead to exegetical anarchy or flights of allegorical fantasy, since Ephraem's thought is firmly grounded in Nicaean orthodoxy and his biblical exegesis is heir to the Patristic

---

[61] Brock, *The Luminous Eye*, 57.

[62] Griffith, *'Faith Adoring the Mystery'*, 20.

[63] *Hymns on Faith* 49:4–5, trans Brock, *idem*, 58.

principle that Scripture interprets Scripture. His is a hermeneutic of intertextuality, and anything he asserts as a spiritual reading must be clearly evident elsewhere in Scripture at a literal level. Griffith is very clear on this point. In 'Faith Adoring the Mystery' he comments on Ephraem's approach to reading and interpreting the biblical texts:

> Nowhere does he discuss principles of exegesis as such; everywhere his methods are clear and evident; he begins with the literal meaning of the text, and then he looks for the spiritual sense encoded in the symbols and types, the names and titles which have the incarnate Son of God as their constant point of reference. In this way the integral, Christian Bible is the constant measure of his thought, supplying the very idiom of his religious discourse.[64]

Ephraem's genius is not so much his approach to biblical exegesis as his expression of the fruits of his insights and contemplation of the texts of Scripture in the language of poetry, with its paradoxes, nuances and allusiveness. Sebastian Brock has written:

> Ephraem's radically different approach is by way of paradox and symbolism, and for this purpose poetry provides a far more suitable vehicle than prose, seeing that poetry is much better capable of sustaining the essential dynamism and fluidity that is characteristic of this sort of approach to theology.[65]

Ephraem's poetic theology cuts its way through the academic approach to Scripture that sees it either as a source of historical information or dogmatic confirmation. The Bible for Ephraem is a treasure-house of spiritual riches, a fount of life for the soul, a banquet of images and figurative language to be teased out and to become nourishment.

---

[64] Griffith, 'Faith Adoring the Mystery', 32.
[65] Brock, The Luminous Eye, 24.

For our journey of faith, Ephraem the Syrian is a master of the spiritual life, whose contemplation of the scriptures was a model of *lectio divina*, and who teaches us that faith is not always *fides quarens intellectum*, but also *fides adorans mysterium*.[66]

———◆———

———

[66] Griffith, 'Faith Adoring the Mystery', 37. Griffith contrasts Augustine of Hippo's search for an intellectual understanding of faith (*fides quarens intellectum*—'faith seeking understanding'), with Ephraem's approach, which he characterises as *fides adorans mysterium*—'faith adoring the mystery'. For a brilliant and comprehensive exposition of *lectio divina* with insights from contemporary literary theories of the processes involved in reading texts and generating meaning see, Studzinski, *Reading to Live: The Evolving Practice of* Lectio Divina.

BIBLIOGRAPHY

Edmund Beck, ed. and trans., *Des Heiligen Ephraem des Syrers Hymnen de Fide*, 2 vols. Corpus Scriptorum Christianorum Orientalium, 154–5, Scriptores Syri, 73–4 (Louvain: Peeters, 1955).

Pope Benedict XV, *'Principi apostolorum Petro'*, Encyclical of Pope Benedict XV on St. Ephrem the Syrian, *Acta Apostolicae Sedis* 12(12) (1920), 457–71.

David Bently Hart, *The Story of Christianity: A History of 2,000 Years of the Christian Faith* (London: Quercus, 2009).

Paul Böer, ed., *Hymns and Homilies of St. Ephraim the Syrian* (West Sedona AZ: Veritas, 2012).

Sebastian Brock, *Bride of Light: Hymns on Mary from the Syriac Churches*, Mōrān 'Eth'ō, 6 (Piscataway NJ: Gorgias Press, 2010).

——, trans., *Ephrem the Syrian: Hymns on Paradise*, Popular Patristics, 10 (Crestwood NY: St Vladimir's Seminary Press, 1997).

——, *The Harp of the Spirit: Poems of Saint Ephrem the Syrian* (Cambridge: Aquila, 3rd edn. 2013).

——, *The Luminous Eye: The Spiritual World Vision of Saint Ephrem* (Kalamazoo MI: Cistercian Publications, 1992).

——, *Treasure-house of Mysteries: Explorations of the Sacred Text Through Poetry in the Syriac Tradition*, Popular Patristics, 45 (New York: St Vladimir's Seminary Press, 2012).

—— & George A. Kiraz (eds), *Ephrem the Syrian: Selected Poems*, Eastern Christian Texts in translation, 2 (Provo: Brigham Young University, 2006).

C. Brockelmann, ed., *Syriac Life of Ephrem, Syrische Grammatik mit Paradigmen, Chrestomathie und Glossar* (Leipzig: Verlag Enzyklopädie, 12th edn. 1976).

H. Burgess, *The Repentance of Nineveh* (London: Robert B. Blackadder, 1853) [Narrative poem on the repentance of Nineveh].

G. W. Butterworth, ed., *Origen, De Principiis* (Eugene OR: Wipf & Stock, 2012).

Hans von Campenhausen, *The Fathers of the Greek Church* (London: A. & C. Black, 1963).

Henri Crouzel, *Origen*, trans. by A. S. Worrall (Sheffield: T. & T. Clark, 1989).

Jean Daniélou SJ, *Origen*, trans. by Walter Mitchell (London: Sheed and Ward, 1955).

Marcellino D'Ambrosio, *Who Were the Church Fathers? From Clement of Rome to Gregory the Great* (London: SPCK, 2015).

Brian E. Daley, *God Visible: Patristic Christology Reconsidered* (Oxford: OUP, 2018).

A Dictionary of Christian Spirituality, ed. by G. Wakefield (Norwich: SCM Press, 1983).

Sidney H. Griffith, *'Faith Adoring the Mystery': Reading the Bible with St. Ephraem the Syrian*, Père Marquette Lectures, 28 (Ann Arbor MI: Marquette University Press, 1997).

John Gwynn, *Hymns and Homilies of St. Ephraim the Syrian* ed. by Paul A. Boer (Scotts Valley CA: Veritatis Splendor Publications, 2012).

——, ed. and trans., *Gregory the Great: Part II, Ephraim Syrus, Aphrahat*, A Select Library of Nicene and Post-Nicene Fathers, Second Series, 13, repr. of 1890–1900 edn (Grand Rapids MI: Eerdmans, 1969) [includes Nisibene Hymns and Hymns on Epiphany].

——, *The Life and Essential Writings of Ephraim the Syrian*, Desert Fathers Series, 5 (Jasper FL: Revelation Insight, 2011).

Mary T. Hansbury, trans., *Hymns of Saint Ephrem the Syrian*, Fairacres Publications, 149 (Oxford: SLG Press, 2006, repr. 2018) [Hymns on the Table].

Ronald E. Heine, *Origen: Scholarship in the Service of the Church*, Christian Theology in Context (Oxford: OUP, 2010).

——, *Reading the Old Testament with the Ancient Church: Exploring the Formation of Early Christian Thought* (Grand Rapids MI: Baker Academic, 2007).

Jérôme Labourt, 'St. Ephraem', *The Catholic Encyclopedia*, v (New York: Robert Appleton Company, 1909).

Elizabeth A. Dively Lauro, *The Soul and Spirit of Scripture within Origen's Exegesis*, Bible in Ancient Christianity, 3 (Boston: Brill, 2005).

Abraham J. Malherbe & Everett Ferguson, trans. and introd., *Gregory of Nyssa, Life of Moses*, preface by John Meyendorff (New York: Paulist Press, 1978).

E. G. Mathews, Jr. and J. P. Amar, trans., *Saint Ephrem the Syrian: Selected Prose Works, Commentary on Genesis, Commentary on Exodus, Homily on Our*

Lord, *Letter to Publius*, ed. by K. E. McVey, Fathers of the Church, 91 (Washington DC: Catholic University of America Press, 1994).

Carmel McCarthy, 'Saint Ephrem's Commentary on Tatian's *Diatessaron*: An English Translation of Chester Beatty Syriac MS 709', *Journal of Semitic Studies* Supplement 2 (1993).

J. A. McGuckin, 'Origen of Alexandria', in *A–Z of Patristic Theology* (Norwich: SCM Press, 2005).

K. E. McVey, *Ephrem the Syrian: Hymns*, Classics of Western Spirituality (New York: Paulist Press, 1989).

J. B. Morris, *Selected Works of St. Ephrem the Syrian* (Oxford: J. H. Parker, 1847) [Hymns and verse homilies on Faith; Hymns on the Nativity].

Robert Murray, *Symbols of Church and Kingdom: A Study in Early Syriac Tradition* (New York: Cambridge University Press, 1975).

Gerald O'Collins & Edward G. Farrugia, *A Concise Dictionary of Theology* (Sheffield: T. & T. Clark, 2000).

The Oxford Dictionary of the Christian Church, ed. by F. L. Cross & E. A. Livingstone (Oxford: OUP, 2nd edn. repr. 1983).

A. Salvesen, *The Exodus Commentary of St Ephrem: A Fourth Century Syriac Commentary on the Book of Exodus*, Mōrān 'Eth'ō, 8 (Piscataway NJ: Gorgias Press, 2011).

Manlio Simonetti, *Biblical Interpretation in the Early Church: An Historical Introduction to Patristic Exegesis*, trans. by John Hughes (Edinburgh: T. & T. Clark, 1994).

David Wesley Soper, *Major Voices in American Theology: Men Who Shape Belief* (Philadelphia: Westminster Press, 1953).

Raymond Studzinski OSB, *Reading to Live: The Evolving Practice of* Lectio Divina, Cistercian Studies, 231 (Kalamazoo: Cistercian Publications, 2009).

Tertullian, *The Five Books Against Marcion*, trans. P. Holmes, Lighthouse Church Fathers Series, 91 (Minnesota: Lighthouse Publishing, 2018).

Paul Tillich, *A History of Christian Thought*, ed. by Carl Braaten (Norwich: SCM Press, 1968).

J. E. Walters, *Hymns on the Unleavened Bread by Ephrem the Syrian*, Texts from Christian Late Antiquity, 30 (Piscataway NJ: Gorgias Press, 2011).

Jeffrey T. Wickes, trans., *St. Ephrem the Syrian: The Hymns on Faith*, Fathers of the Church, 130 (Washington DC: Catholic University of America Press, 2015).

PATRISTICS TEXTS PUBLISHED BY SLG PRESS

Available from www.slgpress.co.uk

SLG PRESS PUBLICATIONS

slgpress.co.uk